BASEBALL LEGENDS

Hank Aaron
Grover Cleveland Alexander
Ernie Banks
Johnny Bench
Yogi Berra
Roy Campanella
Roberto Clemente
Ty Cobb
Dizzy Dean
Joe DiMaggio
Bob Feller
Jimmie Foxx
Lou Gehrig
Bob Gibson
Rogers Hornsby
Walter Johnson
Sandy Koufax
Mickey Mantle
Christy Mathewson
Willie Mays
Stan Musial
Satchel Paige
Brooks Robinson
Frank Robinson
Jackie Robinson
Babe Ruth
Tom Seaver
Duke Snider
Warren Spahn
Willie Stargell
Honus Wagner
Ted Williams
Carl Yastrzemski
Cy Young

CHELSEA HOUSE PUBLISHERS

BASEBALL LEGENDS

LOU GEHRIG

Norman L. Macht

Introduction by
Jim Murray

Senior Consultant
Earl Weaver

CHELSEA HOUSE PUBLISHERS

New York • Philadelphia

CHELSEA HOUSE PUBLISHERS

Editor-in-Chief: Richard S. Papale
Executive Managing Editor: Karyn Gullen Browne
Copy Chief: Philip Koslow
Picture Editor: Adrian G. Allen
Art Director: Nora Wertz
Manufacturing Director: Gerald Levine
Systems Manager: Lindsey Ottman
Production Coordinator: Marie Claire Cebrián-Ume

Baseball Legends
Senior Editor: Richard Rennert

Staff for LOU GEHRIG
Copy Editor: Danielle Janusz
Designer: Diana Blume
Picture Researcher: Alan Gottlieb
Cover Illustration: Daniel O'Leary
Editorial Assistant: Laura Petermann

3   5   7   9   8   6   4   2

Library of Congress Cataloging-in-Publication Data

Macht, Norman L. (Norman Lee), 1929–
    Lou Gehrig/Norman L. Macht; introduction by Jim Murray; senior
consultant, Earl Weaver.
    p. cm.—(Baseball legends) Includes bibliographical references and index.
    Summary: A biography of the New York Yankee slugger whose feat
of playing in 2130 consecutive games earned him the nickname "The
Iron Man."
    ISBN 0-7910-1176-3
    0-7910-1210-7 (pbk.)
    1. Gehrig, Lou, 1903–1941—Juvenile literature. 2.
Baseball players—United States—Biography—Juvenile
literature.   3. New York Yankees (Baseball
team)—History—Juvenile literature. [1. Gehrig, Lou,
1903–1941.   2. Baseball players.] I. Title. II. Series.
GV865.G4M33 1992   91-28902
796.357'092—dc20   CIP
    [B]   AC

CONTENTS

WHAT MAKES A STAR

Jim Murray

No one has ever been able to explain to me the mysterious alchemy that makes one man a .350 hitter and another player, more or less identical in physical makeup, hard put to hit .200. You look at an Al Kaline, who played with the Detroit Tigers from 1953 to 1974. He was pale, stringy, almost poetic-looking. He always seemed to be struggling against a bad case of mononucleosis. But with a bat in his hands, he was King Kong. During his career, he hit 399 home runs, rapped out 3,007 hits, and compiled a .297 batting average.

Form isn't the reason. The first time anybody saw Roberto Clemente step into the batter's box for the Pittsburgh Pirates, the best guess was that Clemente would be back in Double A ball in a week. He had one foot in the bucket and held his bat at an awkward angle—he looked as though he couldn't hit an outside pitch. A lot of other ballplayers may have had a better-looking stance. Yet they never led the National League in hitting in four different years, the way Clemente did.

Not every ballplayer is born with the ability to hit a curveball. Nor is exceptional hand-eye coordination the key to heavy hitting. Big-league locker rooms are filled with players who have all the attributes, save one: discipline. Every baseball man can tell you a story about a pitcher who throws a ball faster than anyone has ever seen but who has no control on or *off* the field.

The Hall of Fame is full of people who transformed themselves into great ballplayers by working at the sport, by studying the game, and making sacrifices. They're overachievers—and winners. If you want to find them, just watch the World Series. Or simply read about New York Yankee great Lou Gehrig; Ted Williams, "the Splendid Splinter" of the Boston Red Sox; or the Dodgers' strikeout king Sandy Koufax.

A pitcher *should* be able to win a lot of ballgames with a 98-miles-per-hour fastball. But what about the pitcher who wins 20 games a year with a fastball so slow that you can catch it with your teeth? Bob Feller of the Cleveland Indians got into the Hall of Fame with a blazing fastball that glowed in the dark. National League star Grover Cleveland Alexander got there with a pitch that took considerably longer to reach the plate; but when it did arrive, the pitch was exactly where Alexander wanted it to be—and the last place the batter expected it to be.

There are probably more players with exceptional ability who didn't make it to the major leagues than there are who did. A number of great hitters, bored with fielding practice, had to be dropped from their team because their home-run production didn't make up for their lapses in the field. And then there are players like Brooks Robinson of the Baltimore Orioles, who made himself into a human vacuum cleaner at third base because he knew that working hard to become an expert fielder would win him a job in the big leagues.

A star is not something that flashes through the sky. That's a comet. Or a meteor. A star is something you can steer ships by. It stays in place and gives off a steady glow; it is fixed, permanent. A star works at being a star.

And that's how you tell a star in baseball. He shows up night after night and takes pride in how brightly he shines. He's Willie Mays running so hard his hat keeps falling off; Ty Cobb sliding to stretch a single into a double; Lou Gehrig, after being fooled in his first two at-bats, belting the next pitch off the light tower because he's taken the time to study the pitcher. Stars never take themselves for granted. That's why they're stars.

Lou Gehrig glumly watches the action from the New York Yankees dugout on May 2, 1939, after removing himself from the starting lineup and ending his major league record streak of 2,130 consecutive games played.

1

THE IRON HORSE IS DERAILED

Rarely does a baseball player make the biggest headlines of his career for a game in which he does not play. But this is no ordinary story, for Lou Gehrig was no ordinary man. Today, more than 50 years after he last swung a bat, this quiet, shy, modest gentleman still stands out above all others as the height of courage, dedication, and decency.

The day of the game was Tuesday, May 2, 1939. The New York Yankees, the best team in baseball, had traveled by train to Detroit to start their first western road trip of the season. Gehrig had managed only four hits, all singles, in the club's first eight games. Playing first base, he had trouble picking up routine ground balls.

In the last game at home, against the Washington Senators, Gehrig had gone to bat four times with men on base and had failed to advance them each time. The Yankees lost, 3–2, and Gehrig carried the weight of responsibility for the defeat. But the thing that bothered him the most was what some of the other players said to him. Not that they got on him; they had

Gehrig takes batting practice one day before the start of the 1937 World Series. During his 17-year career with the New York Yankees, the ballclub appeared in nine Fall Classics and captured the world championship eight times.

too much respect for their captain to ride him or criticize him. It was their words of encouragement that really stung.

"Late in the game," Gehrig recalled, "I scooped up an ordinary ground ball and threw it over to [pitcher Johnny] Murphy covering first base. It was the same kind of play I had made several hundred times in my big league career, just a routine play. But Bill Dickey, Joe Gordon and Murphy all got around me, slapped me on the back and said, 'Great going, Lou' and 'Nice stop, big boy.' They meant it to be kind, but it hurt worse than any bawling out I ever received in baseball. They were saying 'great stop' because I had fielded a grounder. I decided then and there I would ask [Manager Joe] McCarthy to take me out of the lineup."

Almost 36, Gehrig was starting his 15th season as the Yankees' first baseman and star slug er. He had not missed a single game in all that time. Despite colds and fevers, torn muscles and charley horses, blisters, backaches, beanings, and broken bones (every finger on both hands had been broken at least once), he had reported for duty every day without fail. Sportswriters called him the Iron Horse, after the giant steam locomotives that pulled trains across the nation, and the number of games he had played without missing one had reached 2,130. It seemed as if he would go on forever.

But in 1938 Gehrig's batting average had dropped to .295, the first time in 13 years it had fallen below .300. And he had hit *only* 29 home runs and knocked in 114 runs. The fact that these numbers were considered a bad year for the Iron Horse says a lot about what kind of player he was.

All during spring training in 1939, Gehrig had worked harder than the most eager rookie. He was hoping to regain his usual sharpness and stamina. But they did not come. He felt puzzled, dejected, and old.

So, on this morning in May, Gehrig sat in the lobby of Detroit's Book-Cadillac Hotel reading a newspaper, with a decision locked in his mind. He intended to tell McCarthy about it at the ballpark, but when he saw the manager stroll over to the cigar counter, Gehrig dropped the paper and walked over to him.

"Joe, I want to talk to you about an important matter," the first baseman said.

They went up to the manager's room, where Gehrig said in his typical straightforward manner, "I want to get out of the lineup."

"Do you really feel that way?" McCarthy asked.

"Yes. I haven't been any help to the boys, to the team, to you or to myself," Gehrig replied. He then told the manager of the incident in Sunday's game that had clinched the decision for him.

"Fellows like you come along once in a hundred years," McCarthy told him. "You've been a great ballplayer and a vital part of the Yankees. Don't worry about it; maybe the warm weather will help you come around. Whenever you're ready, the job is still yours."

The two men returned to the lobby, where McCarthy broke the news to the stunned sports writers who traveled with the team. They were aware that Gehrig had to come out of the lineup sooner or later. Yet they were shocked by the sudden reality of it.

"Lou has always been a perfect gentleman and a credit to baseball," McCarthy told them. "We'll miss him. But I think he is doing the proper thing."

Unknown to Gehrig, Wally Pipp had been in the hotel while the slumping ballplayer was meeting with McCarthy. Pipp was the player whom Gehrig had replaced at first base for the Yankees almost 14 years earlier.

That afternoon in 1939, Gehrig worked out in the outfield before the game began. As the team captain, he went out to home plate with the batting order, which did not have his name on it for the first time since June 1, 1925. When it was announced to the crowd that Gehrig had taken himself out of the lineup, the Detroit fans gave him a deafening cheer. He lifted his cap as he walked back to the dugout.

During the game, Gehrig sat on the steps of the dugout and watched the Yankees blast the igers, 22–2. It was as if his teammates were utting on a show for the derailed Iron Horse. hey hit four home runs, including one by iehrig's replacement at first base, Babe)ahlgren. In spite of all the fireworks by the New ork bats, an air of sadness hung over the field.

Gehrig did not accept the possibility that he vas finished as a player. Never mind that he ometimes stumbled when he walked, or fell off chair while trying to tie his shoelaces, or vatched the cards fall from his big hands as he layed bridge. There was nothing wrong with im, he believed, that a little more hard work nd some warmer weather could not fix.

But something stronger than he was, something that all the grit and courage in the world ould not beat, had gripped his powerful body. ou Gehrig never swung a bat in a regular-eason game again. And two years later, he was lead at the age of 37.

A local boy who made good: Gehrig was born and raised in New York, the same city where he went to public school and college and starred as a major league ballplayer.

2
A CITY BOY

Lou Gehrig was a city boy all his life. He was born on June 19, 1903, on the Upper East Side of New York City, in an area called Yorkville. His parents, Heinrich and Christina Gehrig, had been among the millions of immigrants who had left Europe in the 19th century seeking freedom and a better life. They had come from Germany but had met and married in New York.

Like his parents, Heinrich Ludwig (as the future baseball star was baptized) was big boned and sturdy, weighing 14 pounds at birth. The Gehrigs had three other children, but they all died very young. So all the love and hopes and dreams of his parents were lavished on young Louie, as Pop Gehrig called him.

Not that Louie was spoiled; far from it. Pop Gehrig was an expert mechanic, and he and his wife were hardworking, ambitious, thrifty people. But there was usually just enough money to live on from week to week, and sometimes there was not enough.

Fiercely proud, Christina Gehrig bristled when anyone later described Lou as a child of the slums who played ball in the streets in torn and ragged clothes. "I don't pretend Lou was born with a silver spoon in his mouth," she protested. "But he never left the table hungry and I can say he had a terrible appetite from the first time he saw daylight. Maybe his clothes were torn, dirty and rumpled after playing baseball and football, but he was always clean and neatly dressed when I sent him off to school."

Neighbors recall seeing the chunky blond boy walking to school each day wearing a blue cap, jacket, and kneepants, his books slung over his shoulder. Even then Lou showed his stubborn drive to be on the job, no matter what. Ordered to stay in bed one day with a high fever, he slipped outside and walked to school. He knew that was where he was supposed to be. The teacher took one look at the youngster's flushed, damp face and sent him home.

When Lou was four, the Gehrigs moved to the area of upper Manhattan known as Washington Heights. Mostly German and Irish families lived there, and he became used to hearing the local youngsters call one another Dutch and Krauthead. Although Lou was bigger and stronger than the other kids, he was shy and lacked the confidence to be a leader.

There was a big park across the street from the Gehrigs' home, and Lou could find any kind of ball game in season. In winter, there were also sleigh rides and snowball fights. Sometimes the neighborhood boys swiped potatoes from vegetable stands and roasted them over trash fires in empty lots. During the summer, they swam in the nearby Hudson River, diving from the steep cliffs. When Lou was 11, he swam the mile-wide river to New Jersey. Pop Gehrig was proud of that feat but boxed his son's ears for taking such a risk.

HIGH SCHOOL OF COMMERCE
1920 NATIONAL HIGH SCHOOL BASEBALL CHAMPIONS

While Lou was still in elementary school, his father took him to a gymnasium so he could build up his strength following several childhood illnesses. By the time Lou entered Commerce High School, he had massive shoulders and thighs and weighed almost 200 pounds. On the playground, he could wallop a baseball farther than anybody, carry a football through a swarm of would-be tacklers, and outrace everybody down the soccer field. He thought of himself as just a sandlot player, though, and did not go out for any school teams.

In fact, the Iron Horse, now remembered for his bravery and dependability, actually ran away from his first game. "Some of the kids had told my bookkeeping teacher that I could hit the ball a mile in the park," he recalled. "The teacher

Gehrig (middle row, third from right) sits for a team portrait during his senior year at Commerce High School. The ballclub won the 1920 New York City baseball championship and later became the national high school champions.

ordered me to show up for a school game. I went up to the stadium on a streetcar. When I got there and saw so many people going into the field, and heard all the cheering and noise, I was so scared I couldn't see straight. I turned right around and got back on the streetcar and went home. The next day the teacher threatened to flunk me if I didn't show up for the next game. So I went."

The future star athlete would be forever grateful to the teacher for giving him a much-needed push. And pretty soon there was no stopping Lou. He went out for baseball, football, hockey, soccer, basketball, wrestling—every sport that his school offered.

There was one problem, however. After Lou underwent a physical exam, his doctors told him he had a bad heart and would have to quit playing sports. In fact, Lou simply had a small heart, which can be an asset to an athlete because it pumps blood more efficiently than a large one. Indeed, some of the greatest long-distance runners have had small hearts.

Lou decided to stick with football and baseball and give up the other sports. On the gridiron, he loved to carry the pigskin; but he also played along the line and was an excellent punter. On the baseball field, he pitched and played first base.

During Lou's senior year, Commerce High won the city baseball championship. The team was challenged by Lane Tech of Chicago to a one-game playoff at Wrigley Field. Lou needed his parents' consent to make the trip. One night at supper, he announced, "I am going to Chicago."

"What foolishness is this?" his mother demanded.

"The whole team is going, but I need your consent," Lou said.

Heinrich and Christina Gehrig talked the matter over long into the night. "You would have thought I was going to Borneo or Zanzibar," Lou recalled. "Finally they gave their consent."

In Chicago, Lou came up to bat in the ninth inning with two men on base and his team down by a run. He belted the ball out of the big league park to win the game. The newspaper stories and the hero's welcome that greeted the teenager when he returned home brought him offers from colleges and stirred up the interest of baseball scouts.

But Lou had other things on his mind besides playing baseball. His father had become ill and could not work. His mother, who was an excellent cook, got a job in the kitchen of a fraternity house at nearby Columbia University. She also hired herself out as a laundress. When Lou was not playing ball or studying, he worked in a grocery store before and after school and all day on Saturday. Then he would race to the frat house to help his mother.

After a while, Pop Gehrig's health improved, and he started working as a janitor. Yet there was never enough money to keep up with the doctor bills and the rent.

Lou wanted to quit school and get a full-time job, but his parents insisted that he go to college. They dreamed of his becoming an engineer or an architect. So Lou accepted an athletic scholarship to Columbia. Still, he waited on tables at the frat house in his spare time and helped his mother with her chores. He was aware of how hard his parents worked for his benefit, and he vowed to make life easier for them as soon as he could.

3

WELCOME TO THE YANKEES

Lou Gehrig's high school heroics in 1921 attracted the attention of Arthur Devlin, a scout for John McGraw, manager of the New York Giants and one of the top men in baseball. Devlin invited Gehrig to work out with the Giants, but McGraw was not impressed by the teenager's performance. Gehrig was a powerful 18-year-old, with broad shoulders, a strong neck, and big, heavy arms, hands, and legs. But he was very awkward and clumsy in the field, and McGraw had other things on his mind than a klutzy college kid.

Somebody, either Devlin or McGraw, suggested that Gehrig go to Hartford, Connecticut, where there was an Eastern League team, and get a bit more playing experience. The chance to earn some much-needed money before he began college appealed to Gehrig. But he was concerned that if he played professional baseball, he might not be permitted to play for Columbia.

"Lots of college players do it every summer," he was told. "Play under a name like Lou Lewis and nobody will know the difference."

*923, Gehrig's only sea-
with the Columbia
ersity Lions baseball
n, he pitched and
ed first base and the
ield.*

Trusting this advice, Gehrig went to Hartford. He played first base in 12 games and hit .261, but he was not at all pleased. Feeling lonely and homesick, he went to a park one day and sat down. When he looked up, he saw Andy Coakley, the Columbia baseball coach, standing in front of him. Somebody had tipped off Coakley that Lou Lewis was really the prize prospect Lou Gehrig.

Coakley explained to Gehrig that he could be barred from playing for Columbia because he had signed a contract. The young man, ready to quit the Eastern League for any good reason, went home to New York and his mother's cooking. A short time later, the schools that were to play against Columbia decided to penalize Gehrig for joining the Eastern League. He was told that he had to sit out his freshman year; he would have to wait until he was a sophomore before he could suit up for the football and baseball teams.

Columbia fielded a fair football squad in 1922, Gehrig's second year at college. He played tackle and in the backfield, but he did not prove to be a gridiron star. The following spring, however, he swung a mighty bat, hitting home runs that endangered windows and pedestrians far from the diamond. He was also the Lions' ace pitcher, once striking out 17 batters in a game. Whenever it was not his turn on the mound, he played first base or the outfield.

Gehrig considered sports to be simply an after-school activity. But his thinking began to change when his mother fell ill with double pneumonia. The years of strenuous labor for long hours had worn her down. The Gehrigs found themselves five months behind with the rent.

Meanwhile, New York Yankees outfielder Babe Ruth had just changed baseball. He had hit an astounding 54 home runs in 1920, more than any other *team* in the American League, and 59 in 1921. Suddenly, every scout was looking for powerful young sluggers, and Lou Gehrig certainly fit the bill. When the Yankees offered him a contract for $3,500 for the rest of the 1923 season, it seemed like all the money in the world to him.

Gehrig's parents were not happy to see him drop out of school after they had worked so hard for him to get an education. But their 20-year-old son looked at the matter in a different light. "Mom and Dad have made enough sacrifices for me," he told a reporter. "Mom's been slaving to put a young ox like me through college. It's about time that I carry the load and take care of them."

Miller Huggins, the Yankees manager, was the right man for the uncertain rookie. Huggins was patient but firm, and he took an immediate liking to the modest youngster. For Gehrig, Huggins was a man of authority, someone he could willingly respect and obey.

In signing with the Yankees, Gehrig was joining a ballclub that had won two straight American League pennants. But the team was also becoming a group of hard-to-handle stars,

Gehrig rips into a pitch at Columbia University's South Field in 1923. He batted 63 times during the 19-game season and hit .444, collected seven home runs, and posted an eye-popping .937 slugging percentage.

Miller Huggins, who managed the New York Yankees from 1918 through 1929, was more responsible than any other person in baseball for molding Gehrig into a top-flight ballplayer.

led by the biggest showman of them all, Babe Ruth. Yankee Stadium, the largest and grandest ballpark in the land, had just opened that April.

Gehrig worked out as a pitcher, a first baseman, and an outfielder, but he looked ragged at every position. At bat, however, he impressed even Ruth. "That kid sure can bust 'em," the Babe admitted.

Gehrig's parents knew nothing about baseball, and their first visit to Yankee Stadium left them very bewildered. They arrived after batting practice and looked for their son all during the game, but they never saw him. At supper that night, the senior Gehrig indignantly asked where Lou had been hiding.

"I was sitting on the bench, Pop. That's why you didn't see me."

"What kind of bummer's business is that, Pop wanted to know, "where they pay a man $400 a month for sitting on the bench?"

Gehrig got off the bench now and then. On June 15, he played first base in the ninth inning and fielded his first grounder successfully. Three days later, he had his first chance at bat as a pinch-hitter. After lashing a hot foul down the first-base line, he struck out. In St. Louis on July 7, he connected for his first big league hit, a single.

Huggins knew the big rookie needed playing time, so he sent Gehrig to Hartford to learn how to play first base. Gehrig's second stay in the Connecticut capital started out as bad as his first. "The first two weeks were terrible," he recalled. "I couldn't hit. I couldn't field, and I decided to quit again."

The Yankees got wind of his decision and sent Paul Krichell, the scout who had signed

Gehrig, to talk to the homesick slugger. Krichell assured him that he had a future in the game and left him with this advice: "The most important thing a young ballplayer can learn is that he can't be good every day."

Gehrig came out early the next day for extra practice. He began to hit after that, and he had one big day after another. He even pitched one game, beating New Haven, 6–4. In 59 games, he collected 69 hits, most of them for extra bases. He was batting .304 with 24 home runs in September when the New York first baseman Wally Pipp turned an ankle. The Yankees promptly sent for Gehrig, who started four games at first base and had four hits in one of them.

What would soon become the most feared one-two punch in baseball history struck for the first time on September 27 in Boston. After lead-off man Whitey Witt was safe on an error, Ruth tripled and Gehrig hit his first major league home run. His .423 batting average in 13 games gave American League pitchers a warning of things to come.

The Yankees won the pennant in 1923, and for the third straight year they faced the Giants in an all–New York World Series. Gehrig had joined the team too late in the season to be allowed to play in the Series—unless the opposing manager gave his permission. John McGraw refused to let the hot-hitting rookie play. So Gehrig sat on the bench and watched his team win its first world championship.

Sixteen years later, Gehrig would again be forced to sit on the bench and watch his team win another world title. But in between, there would be many autumn days of glory.

*Gehrig gets into the swing of things at the New York
Yankees' spring training camp in St. Petersburg, Florida.*

4
MAKING THE
TEAM

In the 1920s, a rookie's first spring training with a big league team was often the most exciting and fearful experience of his life. For Lou Gehrig, it was torture. The world champion New York Yankees were clannish and, at best, ignored rookies on and off the field. Every team member considered newcomers a threat to take the job of one of the regulars: a pal they played cards with, a roommate, a guy with a wife and kids to feed. They would nail a rookie's shoes to the floor (when he was not in them), try to make him look bad on the field, and saw his bats in half.

The sportswriters did not like Gehrig. He was nervous when they fired questions at him, and all he could do was stammer out a few words. He was no good for a story.

After practice, Gehrig was often alone. He had come to New Orleans, the Yankees' spring training site, with $14 in his pocket, and it had to last him six weeks because nobody was paid until the season started. When the others went out to dinner or the movies, he walked the streets. Even if he had the money, he would have found it difficult to spend it on a good time. It was not his nature to spend money freely.

Hartford Senators manager Paddy O'Connor stands alongside Gehrig, who played 12 games for the Eastern League team in 1921 and 59 games in 1923.

As Gehrig's finances shrank, he looked for a job as a dishwasher or soda jerk to tide him over. A writer who learned of Gehrig's plans told Miller Huggins, who advanced the first baseman some money and arranged for him to share a tiny hotel room with two other players.

Discovering that one of his roommates, catcher Benny Bengough, was also close to broke, Gehrig suggested they make some fast money by working as waiters in a fancy restaurant. They went out and found an expensive looking place and went in the entrance. They were headed for the kitchen when Gehrig spotted four Yankee stars enjoying a feast. He spun Bengough around and pushed him out the door. Relieved that their teammates had not caught them waiting tables, they abandoned the idea.

At the end of spring training, Gehrig was sent back to Hartford for more experience. He had a big year, hitting .369 with 40 doubles, 13 triples, and 37 home runs. The Yankees were still in the pennant race when they called him up in September, but three losses at Detroit ended their chances. Gehrig ended the 1924 major league season with 6 hits in 12 times at bat.

Manager Huggins was almost forced to trade Gehrig to the St. Louis Browns to get pitcher Urban Shocker, whom New York wanted for the 1925 season. But the Yankees managed to make the deal for the four-time 20-game winner without giving up their promising first baseman. Even so, the team got off to a bad start, in part because Babe Ruth had become ill and was in the hospital.

Gehrig sat on the bench and collected splinters for the first month of the season. He nagged Huggins to send him someplace where he could play every day. Wally Pipp was still doing a good job at first base and would not let Gehrig break into the lineup. The manager tried to cool the 21-year-old off by putting him in the outfield for a few games, but Gehrig was clearly out of place as an outfielder.

In late May, Huggins benched Everett Scott, ending the veteran shortstop's playing streak of 1,307 consecutive games. It was an all-time record that seemed unbeatable. Light-hitting Pee Wee Wanninger replaced Scott.

On June 1, a wobbly Babe Ruth returned to action. Gehrig pinch-hit for Wanninger that day, but the Yankees lost their fifth game in a row.

That night, Gehrig was in a sour mood. He seemed to be getting nowhere. The next day, Huggins called him into the manager's office and

The New York Yankees' regular first baseman since the 1915 season, Wally Pipp came out of the ballclub's starting lineup for good on June 2, 1925. Gehrig replaced him in the lineup—and started every one of the Yankees' ballgames for the next 14 years.

Gehrig at the age of 21, shortly before he began his first full season with the New York Yankees.

said, "Well, here is that chance you have been hollering for. You are the new first baseman of the Yankees."

Never dreaming that he was replacing Pipp for more than a few days, Gehrig joined a made-over lineup that featured only three players from the 1924 team. He hit two singles and a double in his first three times at bat as the Yankees snapped their losing streak. Gehrig continued to hit, and he played every day. His only thought was to do well enough to hold onto the job and prevent another man from proving he could do it better.

Gehrig's budding playing streak almost ended after two weeks. He was on second base when Chicago pitcher Ted Lyons threw to second to pick him off. The throw hit Gehrig in the head, knocking him out. When he came to, a coach helped him up.

"Listen, kid," the coach said, "your eyes look glassy to me and you walk as if your knees are made of rubber. Better call it a day and go into the clubhouse."

Gehrig had to struggle to stay on his feet, but something told him he would never get back into the lineup if he left the field. Somehow he managed to remain in the game. Even then, though, he did not believe that he would continue to play every day.

Without a bat in his hands, Gehrig was still a crude, ungainly ballplayer. Huggins and Pipp worked with him daily, teaching him the right way to make the plays. He made many mistakes and was slow to catch on to some things. When Huggins yelled at him for making the same mistake more than once, Gehrig was close to tears. It took him many years to overcome all of his fielding weaknesses; but he never stopped working at them. His willingness and lack of conceit enabled him to become a complete player.

Gehrig wound up staying in the lineup for the rest of the season and hit .295 with 20 home runs. But he still felt as if he was just filling in for Pipp. "It wasn't until Pipp was sold to Cincinnati the following winter that I realized I had made the grade," he recalled. "That was the greatest thrill of my career, the knowledge that I was the regular first baseman of my hometown team. At last I could go to my parents and tell them that I had regular work at good pay so long as I could hit the ball and hustle."

5

BASEBALL'S GREATEST TEAM

None of the baseball experts gave the New York Yankees a chance to finish higher than fourth place in 1926. The ballclub had three untested youngsters in the infield: Lou Gehrig at first base, Tony Lazzeri at second, and Mark Koenig at shortstop. The Yankees lineup turned out to be a package of dynamite, however, that would explode for the next three years.

Led by a slimmed-down, reformed Babe Ruth, who smashed 47 home runs and hit .372, the famed Murderers Row was born. Ruth batted third, Gehrig fourth, and veteran outfielder Bob Meusel fifth. All were .300-hitting long-ball sluggers, and they were capable of driving in 400 runs between them.

One bright May afternoon in Cleveland, Indians pitcher Joe Shaute decided to pitch Ruth and Gehrig outside to keep both left-handed hitters from pulling the ball to right field. The strategy worked. In one inning, Ruth hit a line drive that struck third baseman Rube Lutzke on the shoulder and knocked him over. Gehrig then hit a shot that banged Lutzke on the

the New York
es' famed Murderers
neup in the latter
the 1920s: (from left
) Gehrig, Earle
, Tony Lazzeri, and
endary Babe Ruth.

shin. When Meusel's drive hit him in the stom
ach, Lutzke went down and made no effort to ge
up. The players gathered around him.

"Are you hurt, Rube?" Shaute asked him.

"Am I hurt?" Lutzke groaned. "A guy woul
have been safer in the world war."

Gehrig, still settling in as a regular, hit .313
His 16 home runs and 107 runs batted in woul
be the lowest full-season totals of his career.

The 1926 Yankees edged out Tris Speaker'
Indians by three games to win the Americar
League pennant. In the World Series, Ruth hi
three home runs in one ballgame and Gehri
batted .348, but the St. Louis Cardinals won th
Series in seven games.

Most of the experts were still not convinced
that they were watching one of baseball's all
time greatest teams when the 1927 seaso
opened. But they soon changed their minds. Th
Ruth and Gehrig show produced what wa
known as five o'clock lightning. Most game
began at 3:30 in the afternoon; when the sev
enth and eighth innings came around, it wa
usually about five o'clock. And that was whe
their big bats did the most damage. Ruth toppe
his own major league record by clouting 6
home runs. Gehrig kept pace with him for mos
of the season and finished with 47. Gehrig's .37
batting average and league-leading 175 RBI
earned him the American League's Mos
Valuable Player Award.

Despite stories of jealousy and rivalry be
tween the two sluggers, Ruth and Gehrig wer
never anything but friendly. They were both ou
to win. Gehrig never resented being in Ruth'
shadow; after all, everybody was. Nor did i
bother him when Joe DiMaggio came along i
1936 and got all the publicity.

Wherever the Yankees went, the crowds turned out to see the Babe. It always surprised and amazed Gehrig when Ruth would come back to him and say, "They want you, too," and drag him by the arm out to the train platform. Gehrig never got used to his popularity and did not handle it well. He was ill at ease even with youngsters, which made him seem cold and aloof, while the Babe acted as if every kid in the world was his own.

As long as Gehrig did not have to talk, he was okay. He was happy playing stickball with the neighborhood kids in the streets, using a broom handle and a hard rubber ball. Once somebody hit a ball through a butcher shop window and everyone was hauled off to the police station, Gehrig included.

Ruth and Gehrig were such different personalities they could never be close friends. But they barnstormed together in the fall and went deep-sea fishing, which was Gehrig's favorite way to relax.

The 1927 Yankees won 110 games, a league record that stood for 27 years. Then they swept the Pittsburgh Pirates in a World Series that Gehrig almost missed. His mother was still his best girl, and he did not hesitate to let the world know it. Gravely ill, she needed an operation at

Shortly after the 1926 season ended, Gehrig (top row, fourth from right) and Babe Ruth (to Gehrig's left) played in a series of barnstorming contests in 18 states across the nation. In each of the towns where these sold-out exhibition games were held, the top local players filled out the two stars' opposing teams, the Larrupin' Lous and the Bustin' Babes.

the time of the Series. Gehrig felt it was more important to be by her side than with the team Christina Gehrig and Miller Huggins persuaded him to play in the series.

Gehrig's mother recovered, and she and her husband, who had become avid fans, were back in their regular seats at Yankee Stadium in 1928 That season, the Yankees held off a late charge by the Philadelphia Athletics to win their third straight pennant. Carefree and contented, Gehrig hit .374; he and Ruth each drove in 142 runs.

In the World Series against the Cardinals Ruth socked three home runs in the final game and Gehrig blasted four in the four-game sweep Ruth batted .625, Gehrig .545. It was the most awesome display of power in World Series history.

With his salary rising every year and a growing number of World Series checks in his pocket Gehrig was able to make good his promise of a better life for his parents. He bought them a home in a suburb north of New York City and continued to live with them.

The welcome mat was always out for all the Yankees, and the ballplayers came often to feast on his mother's German-style cooking. When Ruth, Lazzeri, Koenig, and Benny Bengough showed up, there might be a stuffed pig, a turkey, and a goose on the dinner table with all the trimmings. There were plenty of scraps for Offra, the black police dog, and Jidge, the Chihuahua that Ruth had given them. Jidge was the name most players called the Babe, whose real name was George.

The Yankees finished a distant second to Philadelphia in 1929. Gehrig played for weeks with a torn muscle in his back and a broken thumb. During one period, his hand was bruised by a pitch, then he strained his ankle. Favoring the ankle, he developed a charley horse in his right leg. Easing up on the leg gave him a pulled muscle in the other leg. Sliding into home plate one day, he was hit on the head by the throw.

Gehrig also broke the middle finger on his right hand. "Every time he batted it hurt him," teammate Bill Werber recalled. "And he almost got sick to his stomach when he caught the ball. You could see him wince. But he always stayed in the game."

By this time, Gehrig had earned the respect and admiration of players on every team. With his batting average just under .300 on the last day of the 1929 season, he saw Philadelphia third baseman Jimmy Dykes playing deep enough to let him beat out two bunts. The two hits gave Gehrig an even .300 for the year.

But Gehrig did not feel like celebrating. Ten days earlier, Miller Huggins had died. Gehrig gave the Yankees manager all the credit for sticking with him and making something out of his raw brawn, stamina, and determination. They were all the assets that the unpolished Gehrig had brought to the Yankees.

As great a hitter as Gehrig was, he was not a naturally
gifted first baseman. But he improved his defense daily by
learning how to field bunts, play farther away from the bag,
cut off throws from the outfield, catch pop flies, position himself behind the base runner, and throw to the proper base.

6

BREAKING RECORDS

The New York Yankees floundered in third place in 1930, but Babe Ruth and Lou Gehrig never let up. Gehrig hit a career-high .379, the Babe .359; they combined for 90 home runs and drove in 327 runs.

The collapse of the stock market and real estate values in late 1929 cost many players all their savings. But Gehrig, ever cautious, escaped without much damage to his bank account. Salaries were cut; except for Ruth, most top players were earning no more than $6,000. But nobody complained. The Great Depression would soon leave 25 percent of the work force unemployed.

Gehrig was healthy most of the year. Asked for the secret of his stamina, he said, "Nothing to it. Ten hours of sleep a night, a lot of water, a sensible choice of food and you'll never have a day's worry in your life." On game days, he ate a light breakfast and no lunch. He ate plenty of fruit and vegetables and avoided sweets and bread. His favorite indoor exercise was to scatter a deck of cards all over the floor, then pick them

Gehrig has plenty to smile about as he poses with fellow future Hall of Famers Bill Dickey (left) and Lefty Gomez (center) in 1931; that year, the Yankees first baseman batted in 184 runs to set the all-time American League mark.

up one at a time. In the winter, he enjoyed ice skating to keep his legs strong. He never wore a hat or an overcoat, no matter how cold it was.

In 1931, the Yankees welcomed a new manager, Joe McCarthy, who possessed the greatest respect and admiration for Gehrig. Another newcomer, catcher Bill Dickey, became Gehrig's closest friend and his roommate on the road.

The Yankees finished second; their failure to win the pennant was not Gehrig's fault. He batted .341 and led the league in runs, hits, total bases, and runs batted in. His 184 RBIs is still the American League record. He tied with Ruth for the home run crown at 46, losing credit for one round-tripper when a base runner ahead of him failed to touch a base.

By this point, Gehrig had completed six full seasons without missing a game. But that winter, on a trip to Japan with an all-star team, he suffered the kind of injury he had managed to avoid in the American League. A college pitcher hit his right hand with a pitch, breaking a bone

Fortunately for Gehrig, the fracture healed y the spring, and the old lightning flashed gain. On June 3 in Philadelphia, he hit home uns in the first and fourth innings and the ankees led, 4–2. The Athletics rallied, and with wo out, Gehrig dropped a pop foul he should ave caught easily. The batter then doubled, nd the A's took an 8–4 lead.

Still boiling over his error, Gehrig came to bat 1 the fifth and lashed another home run. In the eventh, he smashed his fourth homer of the ame. In his last time at bat, even the Phil-delphia players were rooting for him to hit nother one. He did his best, smacking his hard-st hit of the day to deep left center field. Al immons chased the ball and speared it with ne hand, robbing Gehrig of his fifth homer, a eat nobody has ever achieved in the big leagues. ehrig was the first American Leaguer, however, ɔ hit four home runs in a game.

Three other Yankees hit home runs that day s the team racked up 50 total bases in a 20–13 vin. They took the pennant by 13 games and lobbered the Chicago Cubs for their third weep in their last three World Series appear-nces. In the four games, Gehrig collected nine its, including three home runs. He scored nine uns and drove in eight, batting .529. Cubs nanager Charlie Grimm blinked and said, "I just idn't think a player could be that good."

The thunderous Yankees bats were a little uieter in 1933, although New York scored more uns than any other team. The Washington Sen-tors beat them out with better pitching, though, nd the Athletics first baseman Jimmie Foxx aptured the Triple Crown. Gehrig was not far ehind. He hit .334 with 32 homers and 139 RBIs.

Gehrig and his bride, the former Eleanor Twitchell, stand outside their apartment in New Rochelle, New York, on the morning of their marriage, September 29, 1933.

A dutiful Gehrig helps out his mother in the kitchen. His teammates, especially Babe Ruth, loved to come to the Gehrig home and feast on Christina Gehrig's German-style cooking.

The first All-Star Game was played in 1933 Gehrig was chosen by the fans to play first base he would make the team every year until h retired.

Away from the ballpark, 1933 was the mos important year of Gehrig's life. A few years ear lier, he had been introduced to Eleanor Twitche at a party in Chicago. He had forgotten abou her until they happened to meet again. Gehri had met many women, and he was sometime reported to be serious about one or another, bu there was never anything to it. Mom remaine his best girl. She went with him to spring trair ing in Florida and sometimes on road trips.

But Eleanor was someone special, and Lo courted her throughout the 1933 season. H saw her every day the Yankees were in Chicag and telephoned her every night. Christin

Gehrig was not too happy about losing her son to another woman, and relations between her and Eleanor were not pleasant.

The young couple rented an apartment in New Rochelle, near the Gehrig home, and Eleanor started to decorate it. They planned to be married on Saturday night, September 30, at the home of her uncle on Long Island. But on Thursday night they impulsively decided to get married at the apartment on Friday morning and have a reception Saturday night. Lou called the mayor of New Rochelle, who agreed to perform the ceremony.

On the morning of September 29, 1933, as the painters, carpenters, plumbers, electricians, furniture movers, and custodians paused in their work amid the dust and clutter, the mayor pronounced Lou and Eleanor husband and wife in as few words as possible. Gehrig kissed his bride and then headed for Yankee Stadium, where he went 0 for 4. The honeymoon had to wait until after the last game of the season on Sunday.

Eleanor was the perfect wife for Lou. She encouraged his interest in art, music, and books. She helped him overcome his insecurity and urged him to take his place as baseball's greatest star, as Babe Ruth began to fade. Gehrig was used to ducking out of the stadium through a bleacher exit to avoid the fans and autograph seekers. His wife told him, "Park your car right outside the clubhouse, and if anyone wants your autograph, you sign them. Dinner can wait."

They had no way of knowing how few years they would have together, but they had no reason to doubt that Lou Gehrig's greatest years were still ahead of him.

7

"THE LUCKIEST GUY IN THE ENTIRE WORLD"

During a time when honest men would steal loaves of bread to feed their hungry families, when millions of people lost their homes because they had no jobs, and people stood in long lines in every city for bowls of hot soup, it may seem strange that so many of them would continue to be rabid baseball fans. They would as soon spend a hard-earned 25 cents on a seat in the bleachers, cheering on the home team, as spend it on a meal.

How did the players, well paid for the times at $4,000 a year, feel about their profession? Perhaps Lou Gehrig summed it up best in a talk he gave at a forum of civic and business leaders in New York. He said, "I do feel we contribute to the spirit of the country and its mental attitude toward life. . . . It would be a dull place if everyone was a salesman, a contractor or a politician."

Gehrig had not missed a game since he had pinch-hit on June 1, 1925. But nobody kept track of those statistics at that time, including Gehrig. So it came as a surprise to him when a

...g in his next-to-last Series, Gehrig ...s home plate after ...g the ball out of the ...rounds in Game 4 of ...37 Fall Classic. The ...run was the 10th— ...st—he ever hit in ...Series competition, ...put him ahead of Ruth for most career ...RBIs, with 34.

reporter suggested that he was closing in on Everett Scott's record of 1,307 games. A check of the records revealed that the Iron Horse would break the mark sometime in August 1934.

As the streak grew, it became more of a driving force to Gehrig. On the way to Washington, D.C., in June, the Yankees played an exhibition game in Norfolk, Virginia. A young pitcher threw a fastball that knocked Gehrig unconscious. He was taken to a hospital, but there was no fracture, just a big bump.

"Some of my friends advised me to rest for a week or so," he said. "I felt I had to go right back in, so there wouldn't be a chance of my becoming plate shy."

Wearing a bigger cap borrowed from Ruth to cover the bump (ballplayers did not begin to wear batting helmets until the 1950s), Gehrig hit three triples the next day. Rain washed out the game, however, and canceled the hits.

On July 13, Gehrig thought he had a cold in his back, or maybe it was lumbago, a form of rheumatism. The pain was killing him. He singled his first time at bat but stumbled going to first base and barely made it. One inning later, he left the game. The next day he could hardly move.

To keep his playing streak alive, Gehrig asked Joe McCarthy to let him lead off in the first inning. He singled, then left the game. Thereafter, he did not play every complete game. If the Yankees were far ahead or way behind and he was not feeling well, he might sit down in the late innings.

On August 17, 1934, in St. Louis, Gehrig set the new mark for endurance by playing in his 1,308th consecutive game. He always admitted that luck played a part in the record. One day in Boston, a runner collided with him. The muscles in Gehrig's right shoulder were slightly torn. It would have been impossible for him to play the next day. But it rained, and the day after was a travel day. By the time the ballclub got to St. Louis, he was able to play.

If there was any pressure on Gehrig as a result of the streak, he never showed it. He won the Triple Crown in 1934, leading the league in batting average (.363), home runs (49), and runs batted in (165). Babe Ruth, aging and over-weight, puffed through his last year with the Yankees, who finished second to Detroit.

The writers kidded Gehrig for running after every ball and giving every play the old college try. His reply was, "My success came from one word—hustle. There is no excuse for a player not hustling. Every player owes it to himself, his club, and to the public to hustle every minute he is on the ball field. And that goes for the star as much as for the kid who is fighting to get a regu-lar job. . . . If I have achieved any success on the diamond it has been because I have been willing to give everything the old college try."

In the winter of 1934, Gehrig and his wife went with an all-star team to Japan. From there, they went on to Egypt and Europe. Later, there was speculation that he may have picked up some kind of infection while swimming in Egyptian waters.

The Yankees came in second again in 1935, as Gehrig carried the slugging burden on his broad shoulders. Then along came Joe Di-Maggio, and a new one-two punch was born to terrorize American League pitchers. Gehrig led the league in 1936 with 49 home runs and 167

Joe DiMaggio, who became the New York Yankees' newest star when he joined the ballclub in 1936, helps Gehrig get ready for the upcoming baseball season.

Gehrig prepares for his acting debut in the 1938 movie Rawhide, *in which he played the role of an urban cowboy.*

runs scored while batting .354, and New York won the first of four straight world championships. He was again named the American League's most valuable player.

After another banner year in which he hit .351 with 37 home runs and 159 RBIs, Gehrig signed a 1938 contract for $39,000, his highest salary.

That winter, the ballplayer went to Hollywood and starred in a western movie, *Rawhide*. It was not a very good picture, and Gehrig was not much of an actor.

At the movie's premiere, during spring training in St. Petersburg, Florida, in March 1938, Gehrig had to make a short speech after the film was shown. Later that night, sitting with his family and a few friends, he said, "I have everything a man could wish for—success and happiness. I've got the grandest girl in the world for a wife, wonderful parents, loyal and fine friends. I've just signed a good contract and have money and securities in the bank. I'm on top of the world. Folks, I think I am the luckiest guy in the entire world. I don't really know what I have done to deserve so many good breaks."

Gehrig completed exactly 13 years as the Yankees first baseman by playing in his 2,000th consecutive game on May 31, 1938. That morning, his wife suggested that he not go to the game.

"Skip it?" he asked. "I can't do that. They've got a ceremony planned and things like that."

"So what?" she said. "Think how they'll remember a streak that stopped at 1,999 games. That's a lot more memorable than 2,000. All they'll do today is hang a horseshoe of flowers around your neck."

She was mistaken about his record being forgotten but correct about the flowers. When Gehrig came home that evening, he was wearing a horseshoe of flowers around his neck.

But he was not the same old Lou. He had gotten off to a slow start that spring and was not hitting. By July 1, opposing players noticed that he walked and ran like an old man. Pitchers observed that his reflexes were slower. He swung the bat as hard as ever, but the ball did not travel as far when he hit it. His back bothered him. He got into a fearful slump and fought it in the usual way, by working harder and taking extra batting practice.

One day, Gehrig had four hits in a game and boosted his average to .305. He thought the slump was over. But by the end of the 1938 season he was down to .295. Then, in the World Series, which saw the Yankees sweep the Chicago Cubs, he managed only four singles and no RBIs.

"What's the matter with Gehrig?" became the newspapers' favorite topic. For anyone else, 29 home runs and 114 RBIs would have been an outstanding year. But everybody, including the first baseman himself, expected so much more of Lou Gehrig.

Some people said Gehrig should have taken a rest now and then, that the streak had taken a toll. Others shrugged; after all, most athletes begin to slide when they reach the age of 35. The guy bats in 114 runs and scores 115," Manager Joe McCarthy said, "and everybody asks what's the matter with him. I wish I had more players on this club that would be so far off in their play."

One of the most memorable occasions in baseball history: Gehrig is honored by a crowd of more than 60,000 at Yankee Stadium as he bids farewell to the sport on July 4, 1939.

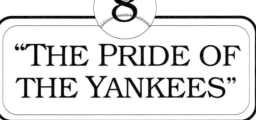

8

"THE PRIDE OF THE YANKEES"

Lou Gehrig took a $4,000 cut in salary, to $35,000, in 1939 and did not complain. Determined to bounce back, he took long walks and went fishing and ice skating. It was his wife, Eleanor, who first noticed that he fell a few times on the ice, something he had never done earlier. When he stepped off a curb, his feet plopped down as if he had not known the curb was there. A pencil or a book would slip from his hands.

Gehrig would not concede that there was anything wrong with him. He and Eleanor went to Florida early to get a head start on spring training. But it was discouraging to him when he swung the bat with all his might and popped up weakly to the infield. Lazy grounders rolled by him at first base as if he were not even there.

On the way north, Gehrig hit three home runs in a game at Norfolk, and everybody said the Iron Horse was back on track. But he never made another extra-base hit.

A week later, the Yankees played at Washington, D.C. Gehrig failed to hit in three games. A 14-year-old fan named Gil Dunn was

Carrying on like a fearless champion, Gehrig enter-tains his Yankees team-mates only days after learning that he has amyo-trophic lateral sclerosis, an incurable form of infantile paralysis that attacks the central nervous system.

at one of those games and remembered it 50 years later: "After the game I was outside the stadium and Gehrig came out and brushed right by the boys asking for autographs and got into a taxi. He was alone, and he looked so dejected. He was walking bent over like an old man, graying at the temples, and I had never seen a man who looked so downhearted. I stood there and felt sorry for him. Here he was one of the great heroes of baseball and I was feeling sorry for him."

A week later the headlines announced: "Lou Benches Himself After 2,130 Straight."

The last time Gehrig appeared in a New York lineup was in an exhibition game at Kansas City in June. From there, he went to the Mayo Clinic in Minnesota for a week of tests. On June 19, his 36th birthday, he heard the results: he had amyotrophic lateral sclerosis, an incurable form of infantile paralysis that is now called Lou Gehrig's disease.

He telephoned Eleanor, who listened tearully as he told her he had a 50-50 chance to ve. "What's more," she told a friend, "he seemed eal cheerful about it. Told me with no more conern than if he had asked about the weather."

When the clinic released the news, medical eople shook their heads and said he had two ears to live at most. Gehrig knew that, too, but hen he landed at Newark Airport the next day, smile dented his cheeks with deep dimples as e answered the reporters' questions. When he almly read the Mayo Clinic report to the ankees in the clubhouse, all eyes were fixed on ne floor, all tongues tied in knots of silence.

The *New York Times* reported on July 4, 939: "In perhaps as colorful and dramatic a ageant as ever was enacted on a baseball field, 1,808 thundered a hail and farewell to Henry ou Gehrig at Yankee Stadium." The old gang om the 1927 Yankees was there. Babe Ruth, ho had not spoken to Gehrig since their famies had quarreled on the 1934 trip to Japan, rapped him in a big bear hug. He received siler pieces and trophies and fishing gear from his eammates, from ushers and office workers and od vendors and writers and fans and even the ew York Giants, who had lost two World Series o Gehrig's Yankees.

Gehrig knew he would be expected to say omething, but he had not written out any peech. He said what he felt: "Fans, for the past vo weeks you have been reading about a bad reak I got. Yet, today I consider myself the ickiest man on the face of the earth."

He thanked the players and managers and lub officials for the honor of associating with nem.

"When the New York Giants, a team you would give your right arm to beat, and vice versa, send you a gift—that's something. When everybody down to the groundskeepers and those boys in white coats remember you with trophies—that's something. . . . When you have a father and mother who work all their lives so that you can have an education and build your body—it's a blessing. When you have a wife who has been a tower of strength, and shown more courage than you dreamed existed—that's the finest I know. So, I close in saying that I might have had a tough break. But I have an awful lot to live for."

The game that followed was watched through thousands of misty eyes. A week later, Gehrig attended his seventh All-Star Game, this time as an honorary member of the American League team. For the rest of the season, he remained with the Yankees as their captain, never giving up the hope of swinging a bat again. Before each game, he limped out to home plate with the lineup card. He shouted words of encouragement from the dugout steps. When he walked slowly along the bench to get a drink of water, the eyes of every silent player followed him. In the clubhouse, he would look a reporter in the eye and say earnestly, "Whatever it is, I'm going to lick this thing."

Fearing that the disease might be contagious, some people urged Gehrig's roommate, Bill Dickey, to let Lou room by himself. But Dickey stuck by his best friend, helping him when he could not tie his shoelaces or strike a match to light his pipe. Watching the daily disintegration of his friend affected Dickey's play, however, and he would have his worst year in 1940.

Gehrig was with the team when they demolished the Cincinnati Reds in 1939 for their second straight World Series sweep, and he tried to join in the victory celebration on the train ride home. But he was too weak. The disease gave him no pain; it just wasted away his muscles, making them unable to perform the tasks they had been designed to do.

The mayor of New York City, Fiorello La Guardia, appointed Gehrig to serve as parole commissioner. He carried out his duties as diligently as he had played first base, putting in six days a week at the office for as long as he could. He was especially hard on young toughs whose criminal activities had caused their mothers a lot of grief.

By the spring of 1941, Gehrig could no longer go to his office. He lacked the strength to write, but he dictated letters for people who had the same disease and had written to him. He urged them to keep up their courage and hope. When a friend called, he was always cheerful and was never heard to complain.

In May, Gehrig had trouble breathing and could not move out of bed. His little black-and-white mutt, Yankee, remained by his side. Gehrig could swallow only pureed food. Eleanor and her mother nursed him around the clock, but it was Lou who kept everyone's spirits up. "Gotta keep playing for the breaks all the time," he told the doctor who gave him vitamin shots every morning.

At 11 A.M. on Monday, June 2, Gehrig closed his eyes. He lingered until 10 o'clock that night. Then, exactly 16 years from the day Miller Huggins had told him, "You take over first base for the Yankees," the Iron Horse died, just 17

Babe Ruth gives Gehrig a huge bear hug during Lou Gehrig Day, July 4, 1939.

days shy of his 38th birthday. Eleanor and his parents were at his bedside.

Back in 1939, the governing members of the Baseball Hall of Fame had waived the rules and had inducted Lou Gehrig without a vote. His uniform number 4 was the first player's number to be retired. An honorary plaque was put up in deep center field at Yankee Stadium. His locker at the ballpark was sealed, and it has never been used again.

One year after Gehrig's death, Academy Award–winning actor Gary Cooper starred in *The Pride of the Yankees*, a movie about the ballplayer's life. Fifty years after Gehrig played his last game, the U.S. Postal Service honored him with a stamp that bears his likeness.

With all his records and achievements on the playing field, Lou Gehrig is remembered most for his dedication, decency, humbleness, and courage in the face of something beyond the control of any person. At his funeral, and on a national radio program, when players were asked to comment on him, they did not talk about his 493 career home runs, his record 23 grand slams, his .340 lifetime batting average, or his 2,130-game endurance record. Joe McCarthy said simply, "Lou was a fine man."

And that said it all.

CHRONOLOGY

1903	Born Heinrich Ludwig Gehrig in New York City on June 19
1923	Signs with the New York Yankees; strikes out in his first major league at-bat on June 13; collects first major league base hit on July 7; hits his first major league home run on September 27
1925	Pinch-hits to start consecutive-game streak on June 1
1927	Wins his first RBI title; receives the American League's Most Valuable Player Award
1928	Wins his second RBI title
1930	Wins his third RBI title
1931	Wins his first home run crown and fourth RBI title, setting the all-time American League mark of 184 runs batted in; named the American League's most valuable player by the *Sporting News*
1932	Becomes the first American League player to hit four home runs in a game, on June 3
1933	Plays in the first All-Star Game ever held; marries Eleanor Twitchell on September 29
1934	Sets all-time record for most consecutive games played (1,308) on August 17; wins the American League's Triple Crown; named the American League's most valuable player by the *Sporting News*
1936	Wins his third home run crown; named the American League's most valuable player by the Baseball Writers of America
1938	Plays in his 2,000th consecutive game on May 31
1939	Removes himself from the starting lineup on May 2, ending his streak of consecutive games played at 2,130; learns at the Mayo Clinic that he has amyotrophic lateral sclerosis (ALS) on June 19; honored at Lou Gehrig Day at Yankee Stadium on July 4; inducted into the Baseball Hall of Fame; becomes the first New York Yankees player to have his uniform number retired
1941	Dies of ALS in New York on June 2

HENRY LOUIS GEHRIG
NEW YORK YANKEES · 1923 · 1939
HOLDER OF MORE THAN A SCORE OF
MAJOR AND AMERICAN LEAGUE RECORDS,
INCLUDING THAT OF PLAYING 2130
CONSECUTIVE GAMES. WHEN HE RETIRED
IN 1939, HE HAD A LIFE TIME BATTING
AVERAGE OF 340.

MAJOR LEAGUE STATISTICS

NEW YORK YANKEES

EAR	TEAM	G	AB	R	H	2B	3B	HR	RBI	BA	SB
923	NY A	13	26	6	11	4	1	1	9	.423	0
924		10	12	2	6	1	0	0	5	.500	0
925		126	437	73	129	23	10	20	68	.295	6
926		155	572	135	179	47	20	16	107	.313	6
927		155	584	149	218	52	18	47	175	.373	10
928		154	562	139	210	47	13	27	142	.374	4
929		154	553	127	166	33	9	35	126	.300	4
930		154	581	143	220	42	17	41	174	.379	12
931		155	619	163	211	31	15	46	184	.341	17
932		155	596	138	208	42	9	34	151	.349	4
933		152	593	138	198	41	12	32	139	.334	9
934		154	579	128	210	40	6	49	165	.363	9
935		149	535	125	176	26	10	30	119	.329	8
936		155	579	167	205	37	7	49	152	.354	3
937		157	569	138	200	37	9	37	159	.351	4
938		157	576	115	170	32	6	29	114	.295	6
939		8	28	2	4	0	0	0	1	.143	0
otals		2163	8001	1888	2721	535	162	493	1990	.340	102

FURTHER READING

Allen, Lee. *Kings of the Diamond*. New York: Putnam, 1965.

Compton, Eric, and Jeff Shermack. *Baseball Stats: What Are They? How to Figure Them. Who's Got the Best*. New York: Scholastic, 1989.

Graham, Frank. *Lou Gehrig: A Quiet Hero*. New York: Putnam, 1942.

Honig, Donald, and Lawrence Ritter. *Baseball: When the Grass Was Real*. New York: Coward, McCann and Geohegan, 1975.

Macht, Norman L. *Babe Ruth*. New York: Chelsea House, 1991.

———. *Christy Mathewson*. New York: Chelsea House, 1991.

———. *Ty Cobb*. New York: Chelsea House, 1993.

Ritter, Lawrence S. *The Glory of Their Times*. New York: Macmillan, 1966.

Robinson, Ray. *Iron Horse: Lou Gehrig in His Time*. New York: Norton, 1990.

Van Riper, Guernsey, Jr. *Lou Gehrig: One of Baseball's Greatest*. New York: Macmillan, 1986.

INDEX

CREDITS
le World Photo, Print Courtesy National Baseball Library, Cooperstown, NY: p. 43; Columbia University,
f Public Information: p. 22; National Baseball Library, Cooperstown, NY: pp. 2, 14, 17, 26, 28, 30, 31, 32,
40, 42, 44, 51, 52, 62, 64; UPI/Bettmann: pp. 8, 10, 25, 34, 46, 54, 56; UPI/Bettmann, Print Courtesy
l Baseball Library, Cooperstown, NY: p. 60

NORMAN MACHT was a minor league general manager with the Milwaukee Braves and Baltimore Orioles organizations and has been a stockbroker and college professor. His work has appeared in *The BallPlayers*, *The Sporting News*, *Baseball Digest*, *USA Today*, *Baseball Weekly*, and *Sports Heritage*, and he is the co-author with Dick Bartell of *Rowdy Richard*. Norman Macht lives in Newark, Delaware.

JIM MURRAY, veteran sports columnist of the *Los Angeles Times*, is one of America's most acclaimed writers. He has been named "America's Best Sportswriter" by the National Association of Sportscasters and Sportswriters 14 times, was awarded the Red Smith Award, and was twice winner of the National Headliner Award. In addition, he was awarded the J. G. Taylor Spink Award in 1987 for "meritorious contributions to baseball writing." With this award came his 1988 induction into the National Baseball Hall of Fame in Cooperstown, New York. In 1990, Jim Murray was awarded the Pulitzer Prize for Commentary.

EARL WEAVER is the winningest manager in Baltimore Orioles history by a wide margin. He compiled 1,480 victories in his 17 years at the helm. After managing eight different minor league teams, he was given the chance to lead the Orioles in 1968. Under his leadership the Orioles finished lower than second place in the American League East only four times in 17 years. One of only 12 managers in big league history to have managed in four or more World Series, Earl was named Manager of the Year in 1979. The popular Weaver had his number 5 retired in 1982, joining Brooks Robinson, Frank Robinson, and Jim Palmer, whose numbers were retired previously. Earl Weaver continues his association with the professional baseball scene by writing, broadcasting, and coaching.